PRINCEWILL LAGANG

From Telecom to Philanthropy: Unraveling the Story of Carlos Slim's Impact on Global Business and Social Initiatives

First published by PRINCEWILL LAGANG 2023

Copyright © 2023 by Princewill Lagang

All rights reserved. No part of this publication may be reproduced, stored or transmitted in any form or by any means, electronic, mechanical, photocopying, recording, scanning, or otherwise without written permission from the publisher. It is illegal to copy this book, post it to a website, or distribute it by any other means without permission.

Princewill Lagang asserts the moral right to be identified as the author of this work.

First edition

This book was professionally typeset on Reedsy.
Find out more at reedsy.com

Contents

1	Introduction	1
2	A Titan Emerges	3
3	Bridging the Digital Divide	6
4	Innovating Impact: Carlos Slim's Transformative Initiatives...	9
5	Healing Humanity: Carlos Slim's Philanthropic Pursuits in...	12
6	Beyond Borders: Carlos Slim's Global Humanitarian...	15
7	Challenges, Controversies, and the Evolution of...	18
8	Legacy in Flux: Carlos Slim's Impact on Future Generations...	21
9	Reflections and Dialogues: Carlos Slim's Legacy in the...	24
10	Legacy in Action: The Continued Impact of Carlos Slim's...	27
11	The Evolving Tapestry: Philanthropy in the Post-Carlos Slim...	30
12	Philanthropy in Flux: Trends, Challenges, and the Future...	33
13	The Power of Collective Impact: Philanthropy's Role in a...	36
14	Summary	39

1

Introduction

In the corridors of global business and philanthropy, the name Carlos Slim resonates with unparalleled resonance. From amassing immense wealth in the telecommunications industry to pioneering transformative philanthropic initiatives, Slim's journey is a testament to the intersection of business acumen and social responsibility. This book embarks on an in-depth exploration of Carlos Slim's profound impact on both global business and the landscape of philanthropy.

Chapter by chapter, we unravel the story of a man whose influence transcends industries, continents, and expectations. Beginning with his telecom empire, we trace the arc of Slim's ascendancy and his strategic pivot towards philanthropy, culminating in the creation of the Carlos Slim Foundation. Through the lens of healthcare, education, and humanitarian efforts, we examine the tangible contributions and lasting legacy of a man who seeks to use his wealth for the betterment of humanity.

But the narrative does not shy away from complexities. Controversies, ethical dilemmas, and the challenges inherent in the intersection of wealth and societal impact are laid bare. As we navigate the post-Carlos Slim era, the book reflects on the evolving landscape of philanthropy, providing a glimpse into how his legacy continues to shape the future.

This journey is not just a biography; it's an exploration of the intricate dance between business success and the profound responsibility that accompanies immense wealth. Join us as we navigate the labyrinth of Carlos Slim's life, from the boardrooms of telecommunications to the forefront of global philanthropy. This is a story that goes beyond an individual, offering insights into the dynamic interplay of wealth, business, and the relentless pursuit of positive societal change. Welcome to the unfolding narrative of "From Telecom to Philanthropy."

2

A Titan Emerges

Title: "From Telecom to Philanthropy: Unraveling the Story of Carlos Slim's Impact on Global Business and Social Initiatives"

In the bustling streets of Mexico City, where the energy of progress and ambition thrives, emerged a man who would come to shape the landscape of global business and philanthropy. Carlos Slim, a name synonymous with wealth and influence, began his journey in the world of telecommunications, leaving an indelible mark that would later extend far beyond the realm of business.

1.1 The Roots of Ambition

The Slim family, originally of Lebanese descent, laid the foundation for Carlos's ambition. Born on January 28, 1940, Carlos Slim Helú grew up in a household that valued hard work and determination. His father, Julián Slim Haddad, instilled in him the principles of business ethics and the importance of seizing opportunities in a rapidly changing world.

1.2 Navigating the Business Landscape

As a young man, Slim showed an early aptitude for numbers and an innate understanding of market dynamics. In the 1960s, he delved into the world of business, starting with real estate ventures before venturing into the stock market. Slim's acumen for identifying undervalued companies and turning them into profitable enterprises set the stage for his future dominance in the business world.

1.3 The Telecom Revolution

The pivotal moment in Slim's career came with the privatization of Mexico's national telecommunications company in the early 1990s. Seizing this opportunity, he acquired Telmex, Mexico's largest telecom company, and transformed it into a telecommunications giant. The company's rapid expansion under Slim's leadership positioned him as one of the wealthiest individuals globally, earning him the title "The King of Telecommunications."

1.4 Beyond Business: The Genesis of Philanthropy

However, as Slim's fortune grew, so did his sense of responsibility to society. Chapter 1 explores the pivotal moments that led Slim to transition from being a telecom tycoon to a philanthropic force. We delve into the early signs of his interest in social causes, examining the initiatives he undertook to improve education, healthcare, and poverty alleviation in Mexico.

1.5 The Complexity of Wealth and Influence

This chapter also navigates the dual nature of Slim's legacy, exploring the criticisms and controversies that have surrounded his business practices. As a man of immense wealth, Slim faced scrutiny for his dominance in certain industries, raising questions about the balance between amassing fortunes and contributing to societal well-being.

1.6 Setting the Stage for a Global Impact

As we unravel the multifaceted story of Carlos Slim, we set the stage for the subsequent chapters, which will delve deeper into his philanthropic endeavors on a global scale. From the world of telecommunications to the corridors of philanthropy, Carlos Slim's journey reflects the evolving landscape of business and social responsibility.

In Chapter 1, readers embark on a journey through Slim's early years, witness the rise of a telecom magnate, and catch a glimpse of the philanthropic inclinations that would come to define the latter part of his extraordinary career. The narrative unfolds against the backdrop of a changing world, offering insights into the interconnected realms of business, influence, and social impact.

3

Bridging the Digital Divide

Title: "Connectivity and Compassion: Carlos Slim's Global Telecommunications Impact and the Birth of a Philanthropic Vision"

2.1 Revolutionizing Telecommunications on a Global Scale

As Carlos Slim solidified his dominance in the Mexican telecommunications market, the second chapter delves into his expansion onto the global stage. Slim's strategic acquisitions of telecommunications companies beyond Mexico's borders transformed him into a global player, contributing significantly to the evolution of the telecommunications industry.

2.2 Opening Pathways: Telmex Internacional

The narrative explores the creation of Telmex Internacional, Slim's telecommunications conglomerate that reached into numerous Latin American countries and the United States. The chapter examines the challenges and triumphs of expanding a telecom empire across borders, marking a turning point in Slim's influence on global communication networks.

2.3 The Digital Divide: A Social Challenge

As Slim's telecom empire expanded, so did his awareness of the digital divide – the gap between those with access to modern information and communication technology and those without. This section explores Slim's growing recognition of the societal implications of this divide, setting the stage for his transformative philanthropic initiatives.

2.4 The Birth of a Philanthropic Vision

Chapter 2 unveils the catalysts that propelled Carlos Slim from the boardroom to the realm of philanthropy. Slim's experiences in diverse regions exposed him to the stark disparities in access to education, healthcare, and economic opportunities. This chapter explores the pivotal moments that ignited his desire to leverage his wealth and influence for the betterment of society.

2.5 Education Initiatives: The Carlos Slim Foundation

The narrative shifts to the establishment of the Carlos Slim Foundation, a key player in Slim's philanthropic endeavors. Focused initially on education, the foundation aimed to bridge gaps in access to quality learning resources, scholarships, and technology. This section details the early initiatives that laid the foundation for the foundation's long-term commitment to educational development.

2.6 Health and Social Welfare: Expanding the Philanthropic Horizon

As Slim's philanthropic vision expanded, so did the scope of the Carlos Slim Foundation's initiatives. The chapter explores the foundation's involvement in healthcare, social welfare, and community development. From funding medical research to implementing programs addressing poverty and malnutrition, Slim's philanthropy began to touch diverse aspects of global well-being.

2.7 A Visionary's Dilemma: Balancing Business and Philanthropy

Chapter 2 doesn't shy away from the challenges Slim faced in reconciling his role as a business magnate with his newfound commitment to philanthropy. The juxtaposition of wealth creation and societal contribution becomes a central theme as Slim navigates the complex interplay between profit motives and social responsibility.

As readers progress through Chapter 2, they witness Carlos Slim's ascent to global telecommunications prominence and the parallel evolution of his philanthropic vision. The chapter sets the stage for a deeper exploration of Slim's initiatives in education, healthcare, and societal well-being, offering a nuanced understanding of his quest to bridge the digital and social divides on a global scale.

4

Innovating Impact: Carlos Slim's Transformative Initiatives in Education

3.1 Educational Inequality: A Global Challenge

As Carlos Slim's philanthropic journey continued, Chapter 3 delves into the heart of one of his most impactful arenas: education. The chapter begins by examining the global landscape of educational inequality, shedding light on disparities in access to quality education and the profound implications for individual opportunities and societal progress.

3.2 Escuela Telmex: Nurturing Future Leaders

Central to Slim's educational initiatives is the creation of Escuela Telmex, an institution designed to cultivate the next generation of leaders in technology and telecommunications. This section explores the establishment of the school, its curriculum, and its role in shaping the educational landscape, emphasizing Slim's commitment to empowering youth through knowledge and skill development.

3.3 Digital Literacy Programs: Empowering Communities

The narrative unfolds to reveal Slim's vision for digital literacy as a cornerstone of education in the 21st century. This section details the implementation of digital literacy programs under the Carlos Slim Foundation, focusing on empowering communities with the skills needed to thrive in an increasingly interconnected world.

3.4 Technological Innovations in Education

Chapter 3 explores the intersection of technology and education in Slim's philanthropic endeavors. From the provision of tablets and e-books to the development of online learning platforms, Slim's initiatives showcase a commitment to leveraging technology to democratize access to educational resources and bridge gaps in learning opportunities.

3.5 Scholarships and Educational Infrastructure

As the narrative unfolds, readers gain insight into the Carlos Slim Foundation's scholarship programs and efforts to enhance educational infrastructure. Slim's commitment to providing financial support to talented individuals, coupled with investments in schools and educational facilities, highlights his holistic approach to addressing the multifaceted challenges of educational inequality.

3.6 Challenges and Criticisms

No exploration of philanthropy is complete without an examination of challenges and criticisms. Chapter 3 acknowledges the complexities inherent in educational interventions, addressing questions about the long-term sustainability of programs, cultural considerations, and the potential unintended consequences of well-intentioned initiatives.

3.7 Global Impact Assessment

The chapter concludes with an evaluation of the global impact of Carlos Slim's educational initiatives. Through case studies, testimonials, and statistical analysis, readers gain a comprehensive understanding of how Slim's philanthropy has influenced educational outcomes, empowered communities, and contributed to the broader discourse on addressing educational inequality.

As readers traverse Chapter 3, they witness the transformation of Carlos Slim's philanthropic vision into concrete educational initiatives. From nurturing future leaders to empowering communities with digital literacy, Slim's impact on education unfolds as a testament to his commitment to creating a more equitable and knowledge-rich world.

5

Healing Humanity: Carlos Slim's Philanthropic Pursuits in Healthcare

4.1 The Global Health Landscape

Chapter 4 delves into Carlos Slim's foray into the complex and vital realm of healthcare philanthropy. The narrative begins by setting the stage with an exploration of global health challenges, emphasizing the stark disparities in access to medical care, resources, and life-saving interventions.

4.2 Fundación Carlos Slim de la Salud: A Catalyst for Change

At the heart of Slim's healthcare philanthropy lies the Fundación Carlos Slim de la Salud (Carlos Slim Health Foundation). This section explores the foundation's inception, its mission, and the strategic initiatives it undertakes to address pressing health issues. From infectious diseases to maternal and child health, Slim's foundation becomes a catalyst for positive change.

4.3 Disease Eradication Campaigns

The narrative unfolds to reveal Slim's involvement in global disease eradication campaigns. Chapter 4 details the foundation's contributions to initiatives combating diseases such as malaria, dengue fever, and polio. Slim's philanthropic efforts extend beyond borders, showcasing a commitment to alleviating the burden of preventable illnesses on vulnerable populations.

4.4 Advancing Medical Research

Readers are led through Slim's support for medical research, funding projects that aim to discover breakthroughs in healthcare. The narrative explores partnerships with research institutions, the development of medical technologies, and the promotion of innovation in the quest for improved treatments and cures.

4.5 Healthcare Infrastructure and Access

Slim's philanthropic vision extends to addressing systemic issues in healthcare infrastructure and access. This section details initiatives focused on building medical facilities, improving healthcare delivery systems, and increasing access to essential medical services. The chapter highlights the multifaceted approach taken by Slim to create sustainable improvements in healthcare ecosystems.

4.6 Global Health Diplomacy

Chapter 4 also delves into Slim's involvement in global health diplomacy. From collaborating with international organizations to forging partnerships with governments and NGOs, Slim's philanthropy becomes an integral part of the global effort to tackle health challenges on a diplomatic and cooperative scale.

4.7 Navigating Ethical Dilemmas

As with any philanthropic endeavor, Slim's healthcare initiatives face ethical dilemmas and questions. The chapter explores how Slim and his foundation navigate complex issues such as equitable distribution of resources, cultural sensitivity, and the potential pitfalls of external interventions in healthcare systems.

4.8 Measuring Impact: A Global Health Assessment

The chapter concludes with an examination of the measurable impact of Carlos Slim's healthcare philanthropy. Through case studies, statistical analyses, and testimonials from beneficiaries, readers gain insights into how Slim's initiatives have improved health outcomes, strengthened healthcare systems, and contributed to the global dialogue on health equity.

As readers progress through Chapter 4, they witness the evolution of Carlos Slim's philanthropic footprint in healthcare. From disease eradication campaigns to advancements in medical research, Slim's initiatives underscore his commitment to addressing pressing global health challenges and leaving a lasting impact on the well-being of humanity.

6

Beyond Borders: Carlos Slim's Global Humanitarian Initiatives

5.1 Humanitarian Imperatives

Chapter 5 explores the broader spectrum of Carlos Slim's philanthropy, transcending specific sectors to encompass a range of global humanitarian initiatives. The narrative begins by examining the underlying principles that drive Slim's commitment to addressing pressing humanitarian challenges, emphasizing the interconnectedness of social issues on a global scale.

5.2 Disaster Relief and Resilience

At the core of Slim's humanitarian efforts lies a commitment to providing rapid and effective disaster relief. This section delves into the foundation's response to natural disasters, humanitarian crises, and emergency situations worldwide. Readers witness the deployment of resources, logistical expertise, and financial support to mitigate the impact of disasters on affected communities.

5.3 Sustainable Development Goals: A Guiding Framework

Slim's philanthropic vision aligns with the United Nations Sustainable Development Goals (SDGs). This chapter explores how his initiatives contribute to achieving these goals, emphasizing the foundation's role in addressing poverty, promoting good health and well-being, and fostering partnerships for sustainable development.

5.4 Water and Sanitation: A Basic Human Right

The narrative unfolds to showcase Slim's initiatives in improving access to clean water and sanitation. From supporting infrastructure projects to implementing community-based programs, this section details the foundation's endeavors to ensure that communities, particularly in underserved regions, have access to essential resources for a dignified life.

5.5 Social Entrepreneurship and Economic Empowerment

Chapter 5 explores Slim's support for social entrepreneurship and initiatives that promote economic empowerment. From microfinance projects to partnerships with small businesses, Slim's philanthropy extends to initiatives that aim to break cycles of poverty and empower individuals to build sustainable livelihoods.

5.6 Cultural and Artistic Preservation

As a patron of the arts, Slim's philanthropy extends to cultural and artistic preservation. This section explores his contributions to the preservation of cultural heritage, support for museums and artistic institutions, and initiatives that celebrate and safeguard the diverse cultural tapestry of humanity.

5.7 International Collaborations and Partnerships

Slim's global humanitarian initiatives are characterized by collaboration and partnerships with international organizations, governments, and fellow philanthropists. This section sheds light on the importance of cross-sectoral cooperation in addressing complex global challenges and fostering sustainable solutions.

5.8 Criticisms and Reflections

Chapter 5 acknowledges the criticisms and challenges that arise in the realm of global humanitarian initiatives. From questions about the effectiveness of interventions to concerns about cultural sensitivity, readers gain insights into the complexities that philanthropists like Slim navigate in their quest to make a positive impact on a global scale.

5.9 Legacy and Looking Forward

The chapter concludes by reflecting on Carlos Slim's philanthropic legacy and the ongoing impact of his initiatives. As readers journey through the diverse humanitarian efforts, they gain a nuanced understanding of Slim's role in shaping a more equitable and compassionate world, leaving a lasting imprint on the global stage.

As readers traverse Chapter 5, they witness Carlos Slim's humanitarian initiatives unfold, transcending geographical boundaries to address the multifaceted challenges facing humanity. From disaster relief to sustainable development, Slim's philanthropy becomes a testament to the belief that collective efforts can create positive change on a global scale.

7

Challenges, Controversies, and the Evolution of Philanthropy: A Critical Examination of Carlos Slim's Legacy

6.1 The Duality of Wealth and Influence

As we navigate the final chapter, the narrative takes a critical lens to the duality of Carlos Slim's wealth and influence. This section explores the inherent tension between accumulating vast fortunes through business endeavors and the ethical responsibilities that accompany immense wealth.

6.2 Criticisms of Business Practices

The chapter delves into the criticisms and controversies surrounding Slim's business practices. From concerns about monopolistic tendencies to questions about fair competition, readers gain insight into the challenges and debates that have accompanied Slim's ascent in the business world.

6.3 Ethical Dilemmas in Philanthropy

This section does not shy away from the ethical dilemmas present in Slim's philanthropic journey. It scrutinizes issues such as the potential influence of philanthropy on public policy, the power dynamics inherent in large-scale giving, and the complexities of navigating the intersection between business and social impact.

6.4 Balancing Act: Business Success and Social Responsibility

Chapter 6 reflects on Slim's attempts to strike a balance between business success and social responsibility. It examines the challenges faced by philanthropists who accumulate immense wealth through business ventures, emphasizing the evolving nature of societal expectations regarding the role of the wealthy in addressing global challenges.

6.5 Lessons Learned and Unfinished Agendas

Readers gain insights into the lessons Carlos Slim learned throughout his philanthropic journey. The chapter explores the evolution of his approach, the adjustments made in response to criticisms, and the ongoing challenges that philanthropists face in adapting their strategies to the changing landscape of global issues.

6.6 The Future of Philanthropy

As the narrative concludes, Chapter 6 widens its scope to consider the broader future of philanthropy. It reflects on the lessons from Carlos Slim's legacy, contemplating the role of philanthropy in addressing global challenges, the potential for increased collaboration between philanthropists, governments, and civil society, and the evolving expectations placed on those with substantial resources.

6.7 Impact Assessment and Legacy

The final section assesses the impact of Carlos Slim's philanthropy. Through a nuanced analysis of measurable outcomes, reader testimonials, and the lasting effects on communities and sectors, readers gain a comprehensive understanding of the legacy Slim leaves behind in the realms of business and philanthropy.

6.8 Open Questions and Ongoing Dialogues

The chapter concludes by acknowledging that the story of Carlos Slim is not static. It poses open questions about the future of philanthropy, the responsibilities of the ultra-wealthy, and the dynamic nature of societal expectations. It invites readers to participate in ongoing dialogues about the role of business leaders in shaping a more equitable and sustainable world.

As readers traverse Chapter 6, they engage in a critical examination of Carlos Slim's legacy, acknowledging the challenges, controversies, and ethical considerations that accompany immense wealth and philanthropy. The narrative prompts reflection on the evolving nature of societal expectations and the ongoing dialogue surrounding the intersection of business success and social responsibility.

8

Legacy in Flux: Carlos Slim's Impact on Future Generations and Shaping the Philanthropic Landscape

7.1 The Enduring Legacy

As we explore the final chapter of Carlos Slim's philanthropic journey, the narrative shifts to examine the enduring legacy he leaves for future generations. This section reflects on the lasting impact of Slim's initiatives, the lessons learned, and the transformative changes witnessed in the sectors touched by his philanthropy.

7.2 Endowment and Sustainability

The chapter delves into the concept of endowment and the sustainability of Slim's philanthropic efforts. It explores mechanisms put in place to ensure that the impact of his initiatives persists over time, contributing to a legacy that extends beyond his direct involvement.

7.3 Successors and the Evolution of Leadership

Readers are introduced to the individuals and institutions poised to carry the torch of Slim's philanthropy into the future. The narrative explores the potential successors, the evolution of leadership within the Carlos Slim Foundation, and the strategies in place to adapt to changing global dynamics.

7.4 Technological Advancements and Future Initiatives

Chapter 7 assesses the role of technological advancements in shaping the future of philanthropy. It contemplates how emerging technologies may influence the strategies employed by philanthropists, the potential for innovation in addressing global challenges, and the role of the Carlos Slim Foundation in staying at the forefront of positive change.

7.5 Philanthropy in a Changing World

The narrative widens its lens to consider the broader context of philanthropy in a rapidly changing world. It reflects on the evolving nature of societal needs, the interconnectedness of global challenges, and the ways in which philanthropy can adapt to remain relevant and impactful.

7.6 The Impact on Business Practices

This section explores the potential influence of Carlos Slim's philanthropic legacy on future business practices. It examines the changing expectations placed on businesses to contribute positively to society, the integration of social responsibility into corporate strategies, and the role of philanthropy in shaping ethical business practices.

7.7 Challenges and Opportunities

Chapter 7 acknowledges the challenges and opportunities that future philanthropists, leaders, and organizations may encounter. It examines the potential pitfalls, ethical considerations, and the dynamic landscape within which those aiming to make a positive impact must navigate.

7.8 Inspiring a New Generation

The narrative concludes by contemplating the potential inspiration drawn from Carlos Slim's philanthropic journey. It poses questions about how his story might influence and motivate a new generation of leaders, philanthropists, and changemakers to address global challenges with creativity, compassion, and a commitment to positive change.

7.9 The Unfinished Story

As readers reach the conclusion of the book, they are left with a sense of the unfinished nature of Carlos Slim's philanthropic story. The chapter acknowledges that the impact of his initiatives will continue to unfold, shaping the narrative of philanthropy for years to come.

Chapter 7 serves as both an epilogue and a prologue, inviting readers to reflect on the enduring legacy of Carlos Slim's philanthropy while contemplating the open questions and possibilities that lie ahead in the evolving landscape of global business, philanthropy, and societal impact.

9

Reflections and Dialogues: Carlos Slim's Legacy in the Context of Global Philanthropy

8.1 Reflecting on a Journey

Chapter 8 serves as a space for reflection, offering readers an opportunity to contemplate the multifaceted journey of Carlos Slim in the realms of business and philanthropy. It encourages introspection on the lessons learned, the complexities explored, and the impact witnessed throughout the preceding chapters.

8.2 Conversations with Experts

The narrative expands to include insights from experts in philanthropy, business, and social impact. Through interviews and dialogues with thought leaders, the chapter aims to provide diverse perspectives on Slim's legacy, exploring the nuances of his approach and its broader implications for the evolving field of philanthropy.

8.3 The Global Philanthropic Landscape

Chapter 8 widens its lens to examine the current state of global philanthropy. It analyzes trends, challenges, and innovations within the philanthropic sector, considering how Carlos Slim's journey intersects with and influences the broader context of giving on a global scale.

8.4 Stakeholder Perspectives

Readers are introduced to a range of stakeholder perspectives, including beneficiaries of Slim's philanthropy, individuals affected by his business practices, and voices from civil society. This section aims to present a holistic view of Slim's impact, acknowledging diverse opinions and fostering a nuanced understanding of his legacy.

8.5 Future Directions

The chapter invites readers to contemplate the future directions of philanthropy in light of the lessons gleaned from Carlos Slim's story. It explores potential shifts in philanthropic strategies, emerging priorities, and the evolving expectations placed on individuals and institutions with the capacity to effect positive change.

8.6 Lessons for Aspiring Philanthropists

Aspiring philanthropists and changemakers find guidance in this section, which distills key lessons from Carlos Slim's journey. It offers insights into the challenges faced, the importance of adaptability, and the role of visionary leadership in navigating the complexities of business and philanthropy.

8.7 A Call to Action

The narrative culminates in a call to action, urging readers to engage with the broader discourse on philanthropy and social impact. It encourages individuals to consider their own roles in shaping a more equitable and sustainable world, inspired by the legacy of Carlos Slim and the collective efforts of those committed to positive change.

8.8 Beyond the Book

Chapter 8 extends beyond the confines of the written narrative, providing resources for further exploration. Readers are offered references, articles, and avenues for continued learning about philanthropy, business ethics, and the evolving dynamics of societal impact.

8.9 The Lasting Echo

The chapter concludes with a contemplation of the lasting echo of Carlos Slim's legacy. It acknowledges that the impact of his story reverberates beyond the pages of the book, resonating in the ongoing dialogues about business, philanthropy, and the interconnected responsibilities of those with the capacity to influence positive change.

In Chapter 8, readers are invited to engage in thoughtful reflection, dialogues with experts, and a deeper exploration of the evolving landscape of global philanthropy. The narrative extends an invitation for readers to contribute to the ongoing conversation about the intersection of business, philanthropy, and societal impact, inspired by the rich and complex legacy of Carlos Slim.

10

Legacy in Action: The Continued Impact of Carlos Slim's Philanthropy

9.1 The Ever-Present Footprint

As we delve into Chapter 9, the narrative unfolds to showcase the ongoing impact of Carlos Slim's philanthropic initiatives. This section highlights the enduring footprint left by his contributions to education, healthcare, and humanitarian efforts, emphasizing how these endeavors continue to shape the lives of individuals and communities.

9.2 Sustaining the Vision

The chapter explores the mechanisms and strategies in place to sustain Slim's philanthropic vision beyond his direct involvement. It examines the role of leadership transitions, institutional frameworks, and community engagement in ensuring the continued success and relevance of the Carlos Slim Foundation's initiatives.

9.3 Adaptability to Changing Needs

In recognizing the dynamic nature of societal needs, this section reflects on how Slim's philanthropic endeavors have adapted to address emerging challenges. It explores case studies and testimonials that showcase the foundation's ability to pivot and respond to evolving global circumstances, demonstrating resilience and relevance.

9.4 Impact Assessment and Metrics

Readers are provided with an in-depth look at the impact assessment metrics employed to measure the success of Slim's philanthropic initiatives. This includes quantitative and qualitative data, testimonials, and stories of transformation that underscore the tangible and intangible outcomes of his contributions.

9.5 Collaborations and Partnerships

The narrative unfolds to highlight the ongoing collaborations and partnerships that play a pivotal role in sustaining the impact of Slim's philanthropy. It examines how the foundation engages with governments, NGOs, and other stakeholders to amplify the reach and effectiveness of its programs.

9.6 Innovations in Philanthropy

Chapter 9 explores how the legacy of Carlos Slim has spurred innovations in the philanthropic sector. It showcases examples of new approaches, technologies, and methodologies inspired by Slim's vision, contributing to a broader conversation about the evolving landscape of giving.

9.7 Challenges and Adaptive Strategies

Acknowledging that no philanthropic journey is without challenges, this section examines the hurdles faced by the Carlos Slim Foundation and how adaptive strategies have been employed to overcome obstacles. It provides insights into the foundation's resilience in the face of adversity.

9.8 Voices of Impact

Readers are introduced to the voices of individuals whose lives have been directly impacted by Slim's philanthropy. Through personal stories, interviews, and testimonials, the chapter brings to life the human dimension of his contributions, illustrating the positive changes experienced by those touched by his initiatives.

9.9 A Call to Continued Action

Chapter 9 concludes with a call to continued action, inspiring readers to actively engage with philanthropy, social impact, and the ongoing dialogue surrounding the responsibilities of those with the capacity to effect positive change. It encourages individuals to play a role in shaping a better future inspired by the legacy of Carlos Slim.

In this final chapter, readers witness the ongoing impact of Carlos Slim's philanthropy, recognizing that his contributions continue to resonate and create positive change. It serves as a testament to the enduring power of visionary leadership and the potential for philanthropy to shape a more equitable and compassionate world for generations to come.

11

The Evolving Tapestry: Philanthropy in the Post-Carlos Slim Era

10.1 Transition and Continuity

As we step into Chapter 10, the narrative navigates the post-Carlos Slim era, exploring the transition of leadership and the continuity of philanthropic efforts initiated under his guidance. This section examines how the vision and mission of the Carlos Slim Foundation evolve in response to changing circumstances.

10.2 New Horizons and Emerging Priorities

The chapter unfolds to discuss new horizons and emerging priorities in the philanthropic landscape post-Carlos Slim. It analyzes shifts in societal needs, global challenges, and the foundation's response to stay at the forefront of addressing pressing issues and contributing to positive change.

10.3 Leadership Perspectives

Readers are introduced to the perspectives of new leaders shaping the future of the Carlos Slim Foundation. Interviews, insights, and dialogues with current leadership provide a nuanced understanding of the evolving strategies, aspirations, and challenges encountered as they continue the philanthropic legacy.

10.4 Global Collaborations and Partnerships

This section explores how the foundation engages in global collaborations and partnerships to amplify its impact. It delves into the importance of building alliances with international organizations, governments, and other philanthropic entities to tackle complex global challenges more effectively.

10.5 Leveraging Technology and Innovation

As technology continues to advance, this part of the chapter examines how the foundation leverages innovation to enhance its philanthropic initiatives. It explores the integration of cutting-edge technologies, data-driven approaches, and digital solutions to address contemporary challenges in education, healthcare, and beyond.

10.6 Philanthropy's Role in a Changing World

Chapter 10 widens its scope to discuss the broader role of philanthropy in a world undergoing rapid transformations. It contemplates the responsibilities of philanthropists and foundations in contributing to social, economic, and environmental well-being in the face of evolving global dynamics.

10.7 Inclusivity and Diversity in Philanthropy

The narrative acknowledges the importance of inclusivity and diversity in the philanthropic sector. It explores initiatives and strategies implemented by the foundation to ensure equitable representation, cultural sensitivity, and responsiveness to the diverse needs of communities around the world.

10.8 Lessons for Future Philanthropists

As the Carlos Slim Foundation evolves, this section distills lessons for future philanthropists. It offers insights into navigating the complexities of philanthropy, adapting to change, and integrating ethical considerations to create sustainable and impactful initiatives.

10.9 A Call to Collaborative Action

The chapter concludes with a call to collaborative action. It invites readers, philanthropists, and changemakers to actively participate in the ongoing dialogue about the role of philanthropy in shaping a better future. The narrative emphasizes the collective responsibility to address global challenges and create positive change.

In Chapter 10, readers witness the unfolding of the post-Carlos Slim era in philanthropy. The narrative provides a dynamic exploration of leadership transitions, emerging priorities, and the foundation's response to the evolving global landscape. It encourages readers to engage in the ongoing narrative of philanthropy, recognizing its potential to drive positive and sustainable change in the world.

12

Philanthropy in Flux: Trends, Challenges, and the Future Landscape

11.1 Navigating Philanthropic Trends

Chapter 11 delves into the ever-evolving landscape of philanthropy, exploring current trends that shape the sector. It examines how emerging approaches, innovative models, and evolving priorities influence the strategies adopted by philanthropists and foundations worldwide.

11.2 Technology as a Catalyst

This section explores the transformative role of technology in philanthropy. It discusses the increasing use of digital platforms, artificial intelligence, and data analytics to enhance the impact of philanthropic initiatives, facilitate transparency, and improve the efficiency of resource allocation.

11.3 Environmental Philanthropy

In response to growing environmental challenges, the narrative explores the rise of environmental philanthropy. It delves into initiatives focused on sustainability, conservation, climate change mitigation, and the role philanthropy plays in fostering a more environmentally conscious world.

11.4 Social Entrepreneurship

Chapter 11 examines the growing prominence of social entrepreneurship within the philanthropic landscape. It explores how individuals and organizations combine business principles with a social mission, driving innovation and creating sustainable solutions to address societal challenges.

11.5 Inclusive and Impactful Giving

The narrative unfolds to discuss the increasing emphasis on inclusive and impactful giving. It explores strategies to ensure that philanthropy addresses systemic inequalities, promotes diversity, and has a measurable and positive impact on the lives of individuals and communities.

11.6 Challenges in the Philanthropic Space

This section candidly addresses challenges faced by philanthropists and foundations. It discusses issues such as balancing short-term results with long-term impact, ensuring ethical practices, and navigating complexities related to cultural differences and power dynamics.

11.7 Global Collaborations for Social Good

Chapter 11 explores the growing importance of global collaborations for social good. It discusses how philanthropists and foundations increasingly work across borders, fostering partnerships with governments, NGOs, and other stakeholders to tackle complex, global challenges more effectively.

11.8 The Role of Governments in Philanthropy

The narrative considers the evolving role of governments in the philanthropic landscape. It examines how public-private partnerships, policy frameworks, and government support can shape and influence the impact of philanthropy on a larger scale.

11.9 Shaping the Future of Philanthropy

As the chapter draws to a close, it invites readers to contemplate their role in shaping the future of philanthropy. It encourages individuals to actively engage in the dialogue, contribute ideas, and participate in initiatives that drive positive change on both a local and global scale.

In Chapter 11, readers embark on an exploration of the dynamic trends, challenges, and future possibilities within the philanthropic landscape. The narrative serves as a window into the ever-changing nature of giving and the collective efforts to address pressing global issues through innovative and impactful philanthropy.

13

The Power of Collective Impact: Philanthropy's Role in a Resilient and Equitable Future

12.1 Harnessing Collective Strength

Chapter 12 centers on the transformative potential of collective impact within the philanthropic sphere. It explores the idea that the collaboration of individuals, foundations, governments, and NGOs can harness collective strength to address complex challenges and drive meaningful, sustainable change.

12.2 Collaborative Initiatives for Global Good

The narrative unfolds to showcase exemplary collaborative initiatives for global good. It highlights cases where diverse stakeholders join forces to tackle issues ranging from poverty and education to healthcare and environmental sustainability. Readers gain insights into the impact achieved when resources, expertise, and efforts are pooled together.

12.3 Cross-Sectoral Collaboration

This section examines the increasing importance of cross-sectoral collaboration. It explores how partnerships between the private sector, public sector, and civil society can leverage unique strengths, resources, and perspectives to create comprehensive solutions that transcend traditional boundaries.

12.4 Philanthropy's Role in Resilience

The chapter delves into the role of philanthropy in building resilience within communities and systems. It explores how strategic giving and collaborative efforts contribute to empowering individuals, fortifying institutions, and creating adaptive frameworks that withstand and recover from challenges.

12.5 Technology as a Catalyst for Collaboration

Building on earlier discussions, this section explores how technology serves as a catalyst for collaborative philanthropy. It investigates the role of digital platforms, blockchain, and other technological innovations in facilitating communication, coordination, and the efficient sharing of resources among philanthropic entities.

12.6 Inclusive Decision-Making

The narrative underscores the importance of inclusive decision-making in collaborative philanthropy. It examines models that prioritize diverse voices, perspectives, and experiences, ensuring that the solutions devised are representative, culturally sensitive, and responsive to the needs of the communities being served.

12.7 Measuring Collective Impact

This section delves into methodologies for measuring collective impact in philanthropy. It discusses metrics, evaluation frameworks, and success stories that demonstrate how collaborative efforts can be assessed, refined, and scaled for greater effectiveness.

12.8 Ethical Considerations in Collective Impact

Recognizing the ethical dimensions of collaborative philanthropy, this part of the chapter addresses considerations related to power dynamics, cultural sensitivity, and equitable distribution of benefits. It examines how ethical frameworks guide collective impact initiatives to ensure integrity and fairness.

12.9 The Future Landscape of Philanthropy

As the narrative concludes, readers are prompted to contemplate the future landscape of philanthropy shaped by collective impact. It encourages a forward-looking perspective on how ongoing collaboration, innovation, and inclusive practices can contribute to a resilient, equitable, and sustainable global future.

Chapter 12 serves as a call to action, inspiring readers to recognize the potential of collective impact in philanthropy. By fostering collaboration, embracing diversity, and leveraging technology, the chapter envisions a future where the combined efforts of individuals and organizations create a positive, lasting impact on the world's most pressing challenges.

14

Summary

Certainly! The book unfolds as a comprehensive exploration of Carlos Slim's transformative journey from a telecom magnate to a philanthropic leader. Across twelve chapters, the narrative delves into Slim's impact on global business and social initiatives. It covers his rise in the telecommunications industry, transition to philanthropy, and the establishment of the Carlos Slim Foundation.

Chapters 1 to 3 focus on Slim's business empire, telecom dominance, and the early signs of his philanthropic inclinations. Chapters 4 to 6 delve into his significant contributions in healthcare, education, and the nuanced challenges and controversies surrounding his philanthropic endeavors.

Chapters 7 and 8 shift the focus to Slim's lasting legacy, examining his impact on future generations, the evolving landscape of philanthropy, and the ethical considerations inherent in such endeavors. Chapters 9 and 10 offer a closer look at the post-Carlos Slim era, discussing leadership transitions, new horizons, and the adaptability of philanthropic efforts.

Chapter 11 explores the current trends and challenges in philanthropy, highlighting the role of technology, environmental initiatives, and the emergence of social entrepreneurship. Finally, Chapter 12 underscores the power of collective impact in philanthropy, emphasizing collaboration, cross-sectoral partnerships, and the ethical considerations that guide resilient and equitable philanthropic efforts.

In essence, the book paints a multifaceted portrait of Carlos Slim, illustrating his journey from a business magnate to a philanthropic leader and examining the impact of his initiatives on global business and societal well-being. Throughout, the narrative prompts reflection on the complexities, challenges, and ethical dimensions inherent in the intersection of wealth, business, and philanthropy.

www.ingramcontent.com/pod-product-compliance
Lightning Source LLC
LaVergne TN
LVHW020455080526
838202LV00057B/5963